HOW TO AMAZE YOUR DAUGHTER

A Firefly Book

Published by Firefly Books Ltd. 2015

English translation copyright © 2015 Firefly Books
Original publication © 2014 Tana éditions, an imprint of Édi8

First printing

Publisher Cataloging-in-Publication Data (U.S.)

Vidaling, Raphaële.
    How to amaze your daughter : crafts, recipes and other creative experiences to teach her how to see the extraordinary in the ordinary / Raphaële Vidaling.
Originally published by Tana Editions, Paris, France, 2014, as Comment épater sa fille.
[144] pages : color photographs ; cm.
Includes index.
Summary: "A collection of creative craft ideas for young girls that are easy to learn and fun to do" -- Provided by publisher.
ISBN-13: 978-1-77085-601-1 (pbk.)
1. Handicraft. 2. Recipes. I. Title
745.5 dc23   TT171.V533 2015

Library and Archives Canada Cataloguing in Publication

Vidaling, Raphaële
[Comment épater sa fille. English]
    How to amaze your daughter : crafts, recipes and other creative experiences to teach her to see the extraordinary in the ordinary / Raphaële Vidaling.
Includes index.
Translation of: Comment épater sa fille.
ISBN 978-1-77085-601-1 (paperback)
    1. Handicraft for girls. 2. Creative activities and seat work. 3. Parent and child. I. Title. II. Title: Comment épater sa fille. English
TT157.V4913 2015   745.5083   C2015-903758-1

Published in the United States by
Firefly Books (U.S.) Inc.
P.O. Box 1338, Ellicott Station
Buffalo, New York 14205

Published in Canada by
Firefly Books Ltd.
50 Staples Avenue, Unit 1
Richmond Hill, Ontario L4B 0A7

Printed in China

Conceived, designed, and produced
by
Tana éditions, an imprint of d'Édi8
12, avenue d'Italie
75013 Paris
www.tana.fr

HOW TO AMAZE YOUR DAUGHTER

CRAFTS, RECIPES AND OTHER CREATIVE EXPERIENCES
TO TEACH HER TO SEE THE EXTRAORDINARY IN THE ORDINARY

TEXT, PHOTOS AND DESIGN
RAPHAËLE VIDALING

FIREFLY BOOKS

INTRODUCTION

"All children are artists. The problem is how to remain an artist once he grows up." This sentence is Picasso's. But what is an artist? Someone who looks at the world with a curious eye, gifted with a creativity that transforms raw material into poetry? Yes, children have this talent, this perpetual wonder that makes them enthusiastic for new experiences, capable of investing themselves in a little project with as much enthusiasm and seriousness as they would if their life depended on it: making soap bubbles or paper airplanes, tying a remote-control motor to a stuffed animal on wheels, or making a skirt of flowers to put around a little doll. Playing is about inventing, testing, letting your imagination and concrete experiences rub up against one another. And, in the end, it's about growing as well. Only while growing up, we sometimes lose our open mind. We throw out bottle caps without seeing the possibility of them being wheels; we no longer pick up feathers on the sidewalk. Sometimes, even, we forget to sculpt volcanoes in our mashed potatoes! That is, we forget unless we have the chance to have children of our own, who remind us not to neglect the most important things: play, fantasy and making wonderful things for the sake of making something wonderful!

This book is a helping hand for parents who haven't lost their inner child, for those who, between the "brush your teeth" and "don't forget to say thank you," will add the essential insight: "Never forget to see the extraordinary in the ordinary!"

TABLE OF CONTENTS

ACTIVITIES
to do together

DOLLS
MADE OF POPSICLE STICKS

MATERIALS
POPSICLE STICKS (SOLD IN CRAFT
    STORES)
PATTERNED ADHESIVE TAPE
SCISSORS
BLACK FINE POINT PEN

HOW TO MAKE

1 Place pieces of adhesive tape on each Popsicle stick to represent the clothes.

2 Draw the heads and legs.

Two little girls can spend an entire afternoon on this project.

You can even draw on both sides — a happy side and an angry side.

BALLERINAS
MADE FROM PAPER DOILIES

MATERIALS
PAPER
SCISSORS

HOW TO MAKE

1 Cut out a circle in the paper. Fold it in half, then in half again for a total of four times. You will end up with a cone-shape.

2 Cut shapes out of the thick edge of the side that includes all the layers of paper, like you would to create a paper snowflake.

3 On another piece of paper, draw and then cut out the shape of the dancer's body. It's easier if you fold the paper in half, since the resulting shape will be symmetrical.

4 Unfold the skirt and cut out a slit that's as small as possible while still allowing the dancer's body to fit through it.

5 Put the body through the slit: the dancer is ready to be suspended.

Legs together and heels en pointe: the body, once folded in half passes through the slit at the waist and holds the skirt in place.

PEBBLE PEOPLE
MADE WITH MIX-AND-MATCH BODIES AND HEADS

MATERIALS

PEBBLES
POSTER PAINTS
A FINE TIP BRUSH
PAINT MARKERS

HOW TO MAKE

1 Pair up the pebbles so each set has a head and a body.

2 Paint the base of the pebbles, keeping some of them in neutral colors to resemble skin tones.

3 Draw in the details with the markers.

Coloring workshop for busy hands.

AN ARCHEOLOGISTS' ICE FLOE
WITH FROZEN ANIMALS

MATERIALS
A CAKE PAN
PLASTIC TOY ANIMALS
BOWL
WATER
BLUE FOOD COLORING
A HAMMER

HOW TO MAKE

1 Arrange the animals in the pan.

2 In a bowl, mix water and enough food coloring to create a nice blue. Cover the animals with the colored water.

3 Place the pan in the freezer and leave until the next day.

4 Using the hammer, try to free the animals from the ice.

CANDLEHOLDERS
MADE OF WAX BALLOONS

It's difficult to fill the balloon with water if you don't thread it fully on the nozzle!

By moving it in a circular motion, you'll be able to coat the balloon with wax up to the top.

As it dries, the balloon will flatten at the base and be able to stand on its own.

The balloon comes out from under the wax very easily.

HOW TO MAKE

1 Melt the wax over a double boiler or in a deep bowl that is wedged into a pot filled with boiling water.

2 Fill a balloon with water by threading the opening to the tap nozzle. Use a clip to keep it closed.

3 Dip the balloon into the melted wax several times. Let it dry on parchment paper. To obtain a thicker (but less translucent) wax sphere, repeat this step several times.

4 When the wax mold has cooled and hardened, take off the clip, empty the water, and remove the balloon. Insert a tea light at the bottom of the candleholder. Repeat these steps to create more candleholders.

MATERIALS

WAX
DOUBLE BOILER
BALLOONS
CLIP
PARCHMENT PAPER

You can either keep the edges jagged or else soften them by turning the holder upside down and delicately pressing down against a warm sheet of parchment paper.

MONOCHROMATIC PHOTOS
OF ODDS AND ENDS

HOW TO MAKE

1. Tidy your room: Gather all those odds and ends that seem impossible to keep organized, and that clutter up the toy box. Sort them by color and put them in jars.

2. When your room is tidy, empty the jars onto the floor and arrange the objects in a harmonious way. Take photos of each color grouping.

3. Put the odds and ends back into their jars, again sorting by color, or glue them onto a background to create a work of art.

MATERIALS

A MESSY CHILD'S ROOM
JARS
A CAMERA

THE ART OF KOKEDAMA
HANGING JAPANESE GARDENS
苔玉

MATERIALS
MODELING CLAY
SMALL PLANTS
POTTING SOIL
PEAT SOIL
SPHAGNUM MOSS
A LARGE BOWL
SOLID BLACK THREAD
FINE METAL WIRE

HOW TO MAKE

1 Soak the modeling clay in water for a few hours so it will soften.

2 While you're waiting, go for a walk, dig up some small plants and collect some patches of moss. Or visit a garden center for these materials.

3 Mix one-third modeling clay, one-third potting soil and one-third peat soil in the bowl to create a uniform and workable paste.

4 Delicately loosen the soil from the roots of your chosen plant.

5 Form a ball of paste around the roots, then wrap with moss.

6 Hold everything together by thoroughly wrapping the sphere with thread, and then make a knot.

7 Fasten the metal wire to the thread or through the sphere so the plant can be hung. Mist with water or submerge the plant in water from time to time.

If you add small figurines,
you can create the planets
from The Little Prince.

A KITCHEN SAND PAN
TO USE FOR WRITING PRACTICE

HOW TO MAKE

1. Pour a few handfuls of salt in a plastic bag. Add a few drops of ink and mix well: the salt should now be dyed evenly.

2. Spread the salt in an even layer in an oven-safe dish. Place it in a 120°F (50°C) oven for 15 minutes to dry.

3. While the salt is in the oven, create models of the letters by writing them in marker on paper cards.

4. The game consists of reproducing the letters in the colored sand with a chopstick. To erase, just shake the dish back and forth without lifting it from the table, like an Etch-A-Sketch!

MATERIALS

FINE SALT
A THIN PLASTIC BAG
INK
AN OVEN–SAFE DISH
PAPER CARDS
A MARKER
A CHOPSTICK

Children will always find a fun use for a bag of colored salt.

SHAVING CREAM PAINT
TO CREATE RANDOM PRINTS

MATERIALS
SHAVING CREAM
A CUTTING BOARD
INK OR PAINT
A PAINTBRUSH
SHEETS OF PAPER
A SPATULA

The Final Piece

1 Spread some shaving cream on the cutting board.

2 Paint on top of the shaving cream with ink or paint.

3 Place a sheet of paper flat on top of the painted shaving cream.

4 Delicately peel off the sheet of paper.

5 Scrape off the shaving cream with the spatula to see the design appear.

29

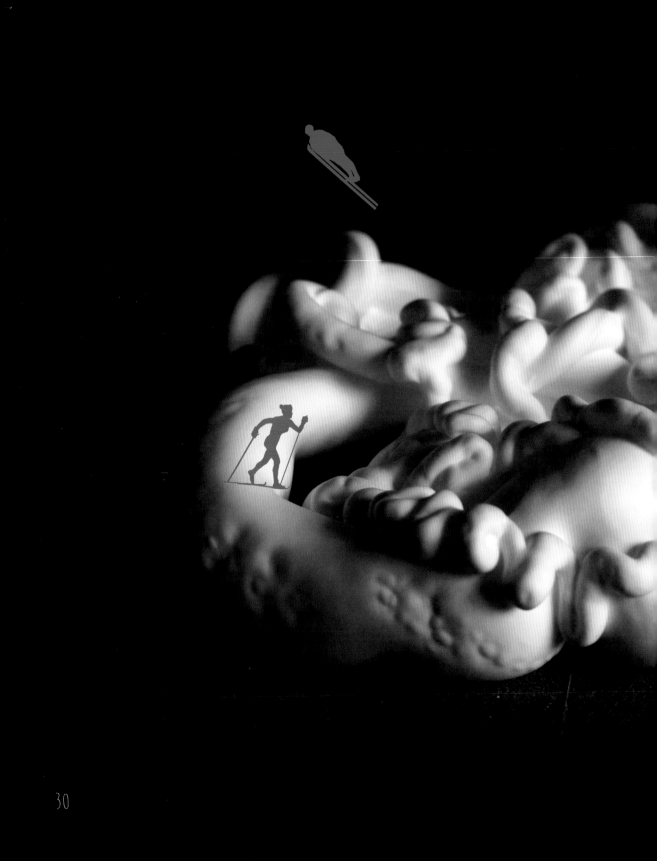

Who doesn't enjoy playing
with shaving cream?

31

LITTLE DRESSES
MADE OF ORIGAMI

MATERIALS
A PIECE OF SQUARE PAPER

HOW TO MAKE
FOLLOW THE STEPS BELOW.

1

2

3

4

5

6

7

8

DECORATIONS
and other little
precious things

MINIATURE VASE NECKLACES
A BOUQUET AROUND YOUR NECK

MATERIALS

MODELING CLAY THAT AIR DRIES
TOOTHPICKS
FINE THREAD
SOME MOSS
SMALL FLOWERS

HOW TO MAKE

1 Model miniature vases in the shape of pots, planters and pouches.

2 Prick the clay with toothpicks to create small holes

3 Let the clay harden as indicated on the package instructions.

4 Remove the toothpicks and string thread through the holes.

5 Decorate with moss and flowers and tie around the neck of a lucky little girl.

REPOSITIONABLE WINDOW DECORATIONS
MADE OF WHITE GLUE

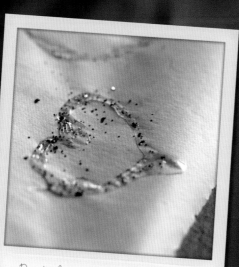

Don't skimp on the glue or your decoration will be too fragile.

HOW TO MAKE

1 Draw a shape with white glue on wax paper. Sprinkle with glitter, if you like. Let dry.

2 When the glue is fully dried, delicately remove the decoration from the wax paper. Apply to a window, lightly wetting if needed. The decoration is so light and smooth that it should stick to the glass.

MATERIALS
WHITE GLUE
WAX PAPER
GLITTER

The wax paper is essential so the decorations are easily removed.

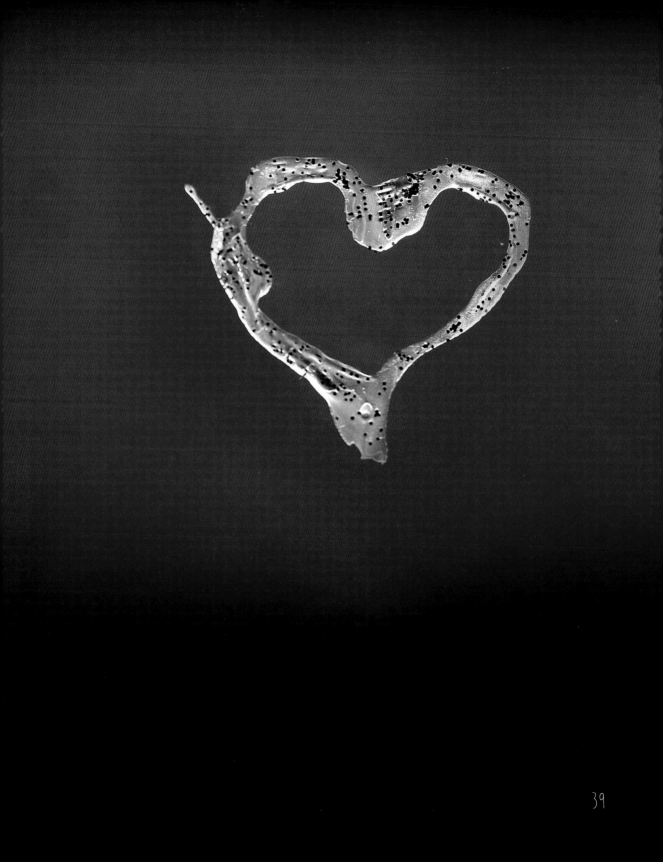

40

A SNOW GLOBE
WITH A RECYCLED TOY INSIDE

MATERIALS

A JAR
A SMALL TOY
STRONG GLUE
WATER
GLYCERIN (AVAILABLE AT THE DRUG
   STORE)
GLITTER
DECORATIVE ADHESIVE TAPE

HOW TO MAKE

1 Glue the small toy on the inside of the jar lid (ideally with a glue gun; otherwise use strong glue from a tube). If the toy is too short, you can glue it on a pedestal made from a Lego brick or a small cap. Let fully dry.

2 Pour in some glitter (not too much) and approximately 1 tablespoon (15 mL) of glycerin. Fill the jar up to the rim with water.

3 Smear the screw top of the jar with glue. Screw on the lid; avoid letting too much air get into the jar.

4 Cover the jar lid and screw top exterior with decorative adhesive tape.

The glycerin is not essential. It simply slows down the glitter as it falls.

COLORED VASES
MADE WITH CUT BALLOONS

MATERIALS
BALLOONS
SMALL GLASS JARS (SUCH AS
    BABY FOOD JARS)
SCISSORS

HOW TO MAKE

1 Cut the balloons about ¼ inch (5 mm) below the openings.

2 Thread the balloons over the glass jars. Push the opening of the balloons inside the jars.

3 Add water to the jars and arrange the flowers.

Children will find it hard to believe that an entire glass baby food jar can fit through the small opening of a balloon!

44

A KEEPSAKE BOX
MADE FROM A DRIED CLEMENTINE

Be careful not to damage the stem of the clementine when cutting it in half.

Monitor the drying of the clementine closely so you don't miss the opportunity to mold your box before it hardens.

HOW TO MAKE

1 Cut the clementine in half. Remove the pulp with a small spoon. Be careful not to damage the peel or the white skin inside.

2 Place on a radiator or a sunny windowsill to dry. After about an hour, it will have hardened a bit. Mold it with your hands into the shape of a little box before it hardens too much. Let it finish drying.

3 Cover the inside with decorative adhesive tape. Thread a small bead onto the stem.

MATERIALS

CLEMENTINE (WITH STEM)
KNIFE
A RADIATOR OR A SUNNY WINDOWSILL
DECORATIVE ADHESIVE TAPE
SCISSORS
A SMALL BEAD

46

WALLPAPER PATCHWORK
PRETTY AND INEXPENSIVE

The children's room version.

MATERIALS
WALLPAPER PIECES
WALLPAPER ADHESIVE
A CONTAINER
A WIDE, FLEXIBLE BRUSH
SCISSORS
A LONG RULER
A TRIANGLE RULER
A CLEAN RAG

HOW TO MAKE

1 Stop in at your local craft or wallpaper store and gather as many wallpaper samples as they'll give you.

2 Prepare the wallpaper adhesive as instructed on the packaging.

3 Spread out the wallpaper samples on the floor and start grouping them according to colors and patterns that match well together. Once you have a grouping that you're happy with, start applying them at the top corner of a wall.

4 Cut a piece of wallpaper at a right angle; apply glue to both the wallpaper and the wall to facilitate the placement. Place the paper on the wall and smooth it with a clean rag, starting at the center and moving toward the edges to get rid of any air bubbles.

5 Repeat these steps for each piece of wallpaper. You can choose to align them next to each other, or allow them to overlap.

The parents'
room version.

It's recommended that you put up the wallpaper patchwork on one wall only and leave the others bare.

A secondary benefit of having a wallpaper patchwork in a child's room: if an area of the wall becomes damaged or drawn on with marker, for example, it's easy to glue on a new piece of wallpaper on top of the damaged one.

51

A MINIATURE TREASURE CHEST
MADE FROM A PILLBOX

HOW TO MAKE

1 Cover the small lids of the pillbox with pieces of decorative adhesive tape that you've cut using a box cutter or hobby knife.

2 Fill the openings with small treasures. You can also bring a section of your pillbox with you on a walk (if it has detachable sections) and collect treasures along the way.

MATERIALS

A PILLBOX (CAN BE PURCHASED INEXPENSIVELY AT A DRUG STORE OR DISCOUNT STORE)

VARIOUS ROLLS OF DECORATIVE ADHESIVE TAPE

A BOX CUTTER OR HOBBY KNIFE

SMALL FAIRY HOUSES
FOUND IN THE FOREST

MATERIALS
PIECES OF BARK
SCISSORS
SEEDS OR DRIED FRUIT
A BLACK MARKER
A WHITE MARKER
A CAMERA

HOW TO MAKE

1 Take a walk in the forest to collect pieces of bark. If the pieces of bark are very hard, soak them in water to soften them: you should be able to cut them with scissors.

2 Cut out small windows and doors in the bark. Add handles made of seeds, and ornaments drawn on with your markers.

3 Go for another walk in the forest to place your doors and windows at the foot of trees or among rocks, looking for natural miniature caves.

4 Take photos of your creations before leaving them behind to hopefully be colonized by fairies or squirrels.

The small doors created before your second walk.

You can also go out into the forest with only your markers on hand and draw on the spot.

ANGEL WINGS
MADE FROM DOILIES

Wings that will even make the biggest troublemaker look angelic.

HOW TO MAKE

1 Create the shape of wings with thick metal wire in proportion to the size of the doilies. Keep the wings closed with the help of thin metal wire.

2 Tear up strips of fabric and use them to cover the metal wire joints to protect the back of the child who will be wearing the wings.

3 Attach two doilies in the top part of the wings with some string.

4 Cut the third doily in half and tightly sew the two halves at the bottom of the wings so they won't fray.

5 Join the doilies from each wing to one another by zigzagging string. Attach the wings to the angel's back by creating loops around the shoulders with string.

MATERIALS

THICK METAL WIRE
THIN METAL WIRE
THREE DOILIES
A PIECE OF WHITE FABRIC
STRING
SCISSORS
A NEEDLE AND THREAD

And when the angel takes off her wings, they will become a beautiful decoration.

for
PLAYING

DOLL CANOES
MADE FROM PLASTIC BOTTLES

MATERIALS
A DOLL
TWO WATER BOTTLES
A BOX CUTTER OR HOBBY KNIFE
DECORATIVE ADHESIVE TAPE
ELECTRICAL TAPE
A MARKER

HOW TO MAKE

1 Sit a doll on top of your bottle to mark the correct placement of the hole. Cut out three sides of the hole.

2 Lift the tab that was created to form the backrest. Cover the backrest with decorative adhesive tape. Repeat these steps for each bottle.

3 Fasten the bottles together at the front and at the rear of the boat with electrical tape. If you wish, write the name of your boat in marker.

The little touch that changes everything: backrests covered with decorative adhesive tape!

Create a trimaran version by using two small bottles around a bigger one.

64

Wanna race?

Hold on tight!

With a child's car seat made of
metal wire for the tiny passengers.

A TABLE TENT
THAT'S BOTH A TABLECLOTH AND A HIDEOUT

MATERIALS FOR A 48-INCH (120 CM) DIAMETER TABLE

TOP FABRIC: 52x52 INCHES (130x130 CM)
WALL FABRIC: 60x80 INCHES (150x200 CM)
DOOR FABRIC: 32x60 INCHES (80x150 CM)
CURTAIN FABRIC: 40x40 INCHES (100x100 CM)
TULLE: 12x12 INCHES (30x30 CM)
VELCRO: 32 INCHES (80 CM)
A USED PLACEMAT
DECORATIONS (OPTIONAL)
SEWING SCISSORS
SEWING MACHINE AND THREAD

HOW TO MAKE

1 Cut the fabric that will be used for the circumference into two long bands measuring 30 inches (75 cm) in width each.

2 Cut out a 4x30-inch (10x75 cm) long strip from one of the bands of fabric for the lintel. Fold this strip in half to obtain a strip that measures 2 inches (5 cm) in width and sew it to the two wall flaps, with Velcro on it, to be able to join them together.

3 Create the door by folding the fabric in half and sewing the four sides, as if it was a pillowcase. Add Velcro at the top. (You can also put a bit on the right, where the door handle is located). Sew the left side of the door to the left side of the wall.

4 Cut out the shape of the window and leave a flap of fabric inside. Sew the tulle to the flap. Add one or two small curtains.

5 To create another window, sew the placemat onto the wall fabric and then carefully cut out the wall fabric in the corresponding shape of the placemat.

6 Add decorations of your choice (top and bottom bands, pockets, mailbox, etc.).

7 Cut out a circle with a diameter of 50 inches (125 cm) for the roof. Sew the walls to the roof. The fabrics can overlap from the back without seams.

The door when it's shut.

Children especially like playing at tying and untying the windows.

BEACH CHAIRS FOR DOLLS
MADE FROM CHOPSTICKS

MATERIALS FOR 1 BEACH CHAIR
ONE PIECE OF 2½x8–INCH (6x20 CM) FABRIC
A THREAD AND NEEDLE OR A SEWING MACHINE
THIN ELASTICS
KITCHEN STRING
TWO CHOPSTICKS
A WOODEN SKEWER
A METAL CUTTING SAW
A DRILL WITH A ³/₁₆ INCH BIT

HOW TO MAKE

1 Cut the chopsticks into two 2½-inch (6 cm) segments (that include the sharp ends of the chopsticks) and two 3½-inch (8 cm) segments.

2 Cut the skewer into one 1¾ inch (4.5 cm) segment and two 2¼ inch (5.5 cm) segments.

3 Drill holes at the extremities of the chopsticks as well as at the 1 inch (2.5 cm) mark (where the sticks will cross each other to create the chair frame).

4 Fasten the two crosspieces with a small piece of string threaded through the holes with a knot on each side.

5 Make a hem on all sides of the fabric (if needed), and sew the band so it creates a loop that goes all the way around, conserving a flap within which the two tips of the seat will be threaded.

6 Thread the skewer sticks into the fabric (to create the top) and in the holes of the chopsticks.

7 Finish by making a knot with the elastic to keep the chair in the seated or folded position.

70

A RECYCLED SHEET TEEPEE
THAT'S EASY TO FOLD AND STORE

MATERIALS

A TWIN SIZED SHEET
FABRIC REMNANT (THAT WILL NOT BE VISIBLE)
DOILIES OR PIECES OF LACE
FOUR PVC TUBES TO PASS ELECTRICAL WIRES THROUGH,
   MEASURING 6½ FEET (2 M) IN LENGTH AND ¾ INCH (2 CM)
   IN DIAMETER (AVAILABLE FOR A FEW DOLLARS)
SEWING SCISSORS
THREAD AND A SEWING MACHINE

HOW TO MAKE

1 Cut the sheet according to the diagram to create three big triangles and two small ones (that will be used to make the front). This pattern lets you get away with not having to create a hem on the bottom or on the length of the flaps that face the front.

2 Sew the doilies or lace using a zigzag stitch in the spots where you would like to create windows; carefully cut out the sheet from behind these spots.

3 Sew the triangles together to create a teepee.

4 On the top and the bottom of each stitch, add a small pocket that will serve to thread the end of each tube (at the top, you can create a sort of mini teepee instead of a pocket).

A variation created by using recycled curtains.

Using doilies or lace goes a long way to fancying up your teepee!

72

THE CLEANEST HOUSE IN TOWN
MADE FROM A LAUNDRY DETERGENT JUG

MATERIALS

A FABRIC SOFTENER OR
    LAUNDRY DETERGENT JUG
BOX CUTTER
PAINT MARKERS

HOW TO MAKE

1 Cut out the door and the windows from the jug with your box cutter.

2 Create a horizontal slit in the corner of the jug that enables you to slide in the piece of the jug that was left behind after cutting out the door. It will transform itself into a removable top story and a deck.

3 Draw on decorations with markers.

74

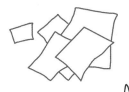

A CARDBOARD HOUSE
FOLDABLE IN A FLASH

MATERIALS
LARGE RIGID PIECES OF CARDBOARD
WIDE, STRONG ADHESIVE TAPE
SCISSORS AND A BOX CUTTER
WALLPAPER ADHESIVE AND A BRUSH
SCRAP PIECES OF WALLPAPER
A GLUE GUN
STRING

HOW TO MAKE

1 Cut out the walls, floor and the roof according to the size of the available cardboard. Make sure to put aside some pieces to create the shingles and the doors.

2 Put together the two side walls and the roof with the adhesive tape.

3 Fold the rear wall into two even parts (to be able to fold the cabin afterward) and attach it to the side walls.

4 Cover the walls with wallpaper as you glue them together.

5 Cut out the shingles from the cardboard you had put aside and glue them on the roof with a glue gun.

6 Cut out two doors from the cardboard you had put aside. Each door should be half the width of the cabin + 2 inches (5 cm), and the height should be the same as the sidewall – 1¼ inches (3 cm). Cover them with wallpaper and cut out diamond shapes.

7 Make a fold at the 2-inch (5 cm) mark to create an edge the length of each door. Sew this edge with string on the inside of the side wall to attach the first door ¾ inch (2 cm) above ground level. Repeat these steps for the second door.

8 Cut out a window in one of the side walls, add some decorations and play.

The shingles give the house a realistic appearance.

You can use wallpaper samples from your local hardware or decor store to decorate your cardboard house.

MINIATURE SHOPS
MADE FROM MATCHBOXES

❀

MATERIALS

SMALL MATCHBOXES
COLORED PAPER
PATTERNED HOLE PUNCHES (AVAILABLE IN CRAFT
    STORES) OR PATTERNED EDGE SCISSORS
BOX CUTTER
GLUE

HOW TO MAKE

1 Cut out a frame in the top of each matchbox.

2 Cover this frame and the inside of the box with the colored paper of your choice.

3 Cut out pieces of colored paper to wrap around each box.

4 Cut out patterns on the edges of each piece of paper with your hole punch or patterned edge scissors.

5 Glue them on the back and the sides of the box to form a railing. Leave the top flap unglued to form an awning.

By putting the small matchbox inside a bigger one, it creates a theater!

You can also attach them together to create an apartment building.

A MERMAID COSTUME
WITH A DETACHABLE TAIL

MATERIALS

AN EXTRA SMALL BRA
TAFFETA
IRIDESCENT
    TRANSPARENT
    STRETCH FABRIC
FABRIC REMNANTS FOR
    THE SCALES OR A
    SILVER MARKER
TWO 16 INCH (40 CM)
    ZIPPERS
SOME BATTING
6 INCHES (15 CM) OF
    VELCRO
SEWING SCISSORS
A TAILOR'S TAPE
THREAD AND A NEEDLE
SEWING MACHINE

HOW TO MAKE

1 Take the child's measurements. For the height, from under the arms down to the feet, and for the width, around the chest + 11/4 inches (3 cm) for the hem – that will give you the size of the piece of taffeta that you'll need to create the dress. You'll need the same dimensions for the piece of iridescent transparent stretch fabric, adding a band of the same fabric that is 4 inches (10 cm) in width and one-and-a-half times the measurement around the chest. Finally, for a larger sized tail (8-10 years old), add 24x60 inches (60x150 cm) of taffeta.

2 Draw or sew scales onto the half of the taffeta that will be used for the dress. Optional: sew some vertical snaps from the chest to the waist as well as at the calves to be able to adjust the costume to fit the child's body.

3 Assemble the two rectangles of fabric (the taffeta and the iridescent fabric), one on top of the other, in such a way as to form a tube with two layers, and include the zippers so you can open the top one from the collar and the bottom one from the feet.

4 Pleat and sew the small band of iridescent fabric onto the bra, and sew the dress onto this.

5 Cut out the shape of the tail twice. Draw or topstitch some veining. Sew in a bit of batting in the middle of one of the sides. Sew the two pieces together, front-to-front, starting with the base. Turn over the fabric as you sew. Continue to assemble the two pieces in the same way. Close at the top and add three small pieces of Velcro: three on the top of the tail (hook side of the Velcro) and three inside the taffeta (loop side of the Velcro).

87

Experiments
and magic tricks

THE MAGIC MILK
THAT DRAWS BY ITSELF

Watch out, it goes fast!

In the blink of an eye, a star or a circle forms and pushes back the colors.

MATERIALS

MILK
FOOD COLORING
A SHALLOW BOWL
A COTTON SWAB
DISH SOAP

HOW TO MAKE

1 Pour some milk into the bowl.

2 Add a few drops of food coloring.

3 Dip a cotton swab into the dish soap and then dab it onto the surface of the milk. The colors will spread apart, like magic.

The explanation: the dish soap forms an invisible puddle on the surface.

84

You can repeat this action on the sides, where the colors are dense. Afterward, you can play at making the paint move on the surface.

AN EFFERVESCENT EXPERIMENT
LIKE A LAVA LAMP FROM THE 70S

MATERIALS
WATER
A TALL GLASS
FOOD COLORING OR INK
LIGHT COLORED OIL
EFFERVESCENT TABLET

HOW TO MAKE

1 Pour water into the glass until it's one-quarter full. Add a few drops of coloring and mix together.

2 Fill the glass almost to the top with the oil.

3 Break the effervescent tablet into four pieces and drop one piece at a time into the water and oil mixture: the tablet piece will fall to the bottom and will produce colored water bubbles that will rise to the top through the oil.

When we pour the oil in, it's already pretty!

86

COLORFUL CRACKED EGGS
THAT YOU CAN EAT

MATERIALS
EGGS
FOOD COLORING
A BOWL

HOW TO MAKE

1 Boil the eggs for 10 minutes, which will hard-boil them.

2 Gently tap the eggs on a hard surface to crack the shells, being careful not to tap them so hard that the shells fall off the eggs.

3 Fill a bowl with water and add several drops of food coloring. Submerge the eggs into the colored water and leave to soak for a few hours.

4 Peel the shell off the eggs very carefully. The colored water will have penetrated in between the small cracks. The inside of the shell is as pretty as the egg itself. Note: the design won't remain intact for very long and will end up bleeding onto the surface.

A JELLYFISH
IN A BOTTLE

MATERIALS

A THIN, TRANSPARENT PLASTIC BAG
SCISSORS
A WIDE-NECKED BOTTLE WITH A SCREW TOP
WATER
A WHITE ELASTIC BAND
BLUE INK

HOW TO MAKE

1 Create a well with the palm of one of your hands and put the plastic bag in it.

2 Pour water into the bag: this will be the jellyfish's head. Secure with the elastic band very tightly, being careful to leave an air bubble inside (this is what will enable the jellyfish's head to rise when you shake the bottle). Note: ensure the head isn't bigger than the neck of the bottle!

3 Cut out small strips from the bag to create the tentacles.

4 Hide the elastic under a knotted strip made from the bag.

5 Insert the jellyfish into the bottle and fill the bottle with water. Add a few drops of ink to color the water, screw on the cap and watch the jellyfish go up and down as you shake the bottle.

Fill the bottle to the brim, otherwise the jellyfish will remain stuck at the top.

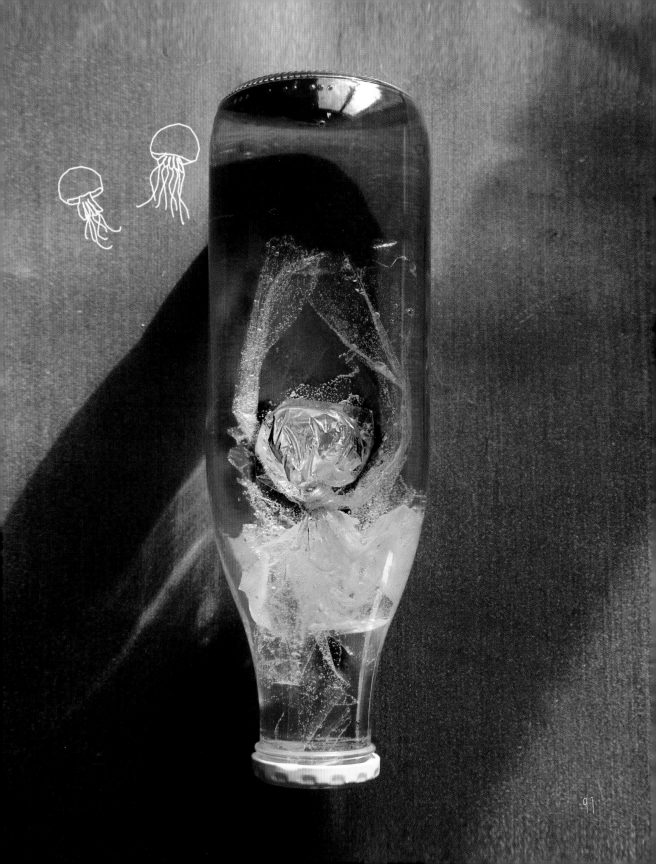

91

A MAGIC FLOWER
THAT OPENS ON WATER

✂

MATERIALS
A SHEET OF PAPER
SCISSORS
A RULER
A PENCIL
A SHALLOW BOWL OF
    WATER

The folding of the petals is an essential step. If you don't follow the instructions, the magic won't happen.

HOW TO MAKE

1 Cut out a circle from the sheet of paper.

2 Trace as many rays as you want petals. (Once you know how to make the flower, you can skip this step.)

3 Cut out rounded ends in a petal shape.

4 Cut out slits along the traced lines of each petal. Stop cutting the slit at exactly the middle point of each ray.

5 Fold back the first petal so that the right side is aligned with the adjacent traced ray.

6 Repeat this step for the rest of the petals. Very important: slide the last petal under the first one.

7 Delicately place the flower on a shallow bowl partially filled with water: it will open instantaneously.

The flower is even prettier when you erase the lines from the rays and decorate it with drawings.

You can write a secret message inside and then put the flower in an envelope and send it in the mail like a greeting card, explaining to the recipient that they must place the flower on water to see the message appear.

You can also hide a smaller flower inside the bigger one.

93

A VERY STRANGE SUBSTANCE
SOLID WHEN YOU MOVE IT, LIQUID WHEN IT'S STILL

MATERIALS
CORNSTARCH
A MIXING BOWL
WATER

HOW TO MAKE

1 Put a few spoonfuls of cornstarch into the mixing bowl.

2 Add a bit of water, stirring to the point of a well-mixed consistency that isn't too liquid.

3 Put both hands in the bowl and play around with the mixture: the sensation is difficult to describe, but it's definitely strange! Try, for example, to create a small tube by rubbing your hands together with some of the paste: as soon as you open your hands, the tube will liquefy and spill through your fingers.

Squeeze hard.

Open your hand: it holds itself together.

Half a second later, it runs through your fingers!

94

Touch a clean finger to these messy hands full of paste and the finger will stay dry! The substance feels like liquid, but the surface is very dry.

95

A RUBBERY EGG
WITH ITS SHELL DISSOLVED IN VINEGAR

HOW TO MAKE

1 Put the egg in the glass and cover it with vinegar. Leave it, without touching it, until the next day.

2 Once the shell is fully dissolved, it will have turned to powder – put the egg under water and the shell will disappear. The inside of the egg will be curiously rubbery and translucent.

MATERIALS

EGG
A GLASS
WHITE VINEGAR

The shell will slowly begin to dissolve away.

The egg will surprisingly remain liquid inside and rubbery on the surface.

The vinegar acts instantly. Its work of dissolving the shell quickly becomes obvious when multiple small bubbles begin to appear.

98

The in-between stage before the total disap-
pearance of the shell is interesting to observe:
the calcareous layer dissolves into dust with
the slightest bit of rubbing.

THE MAGICAL GLASS FULL OF WATER
THAT DOESN'T SPILL WHEN IT'S UPSIDE DOWN

MATERIALS
A GLASS
WATER
A PIECE OF PAPER

HOW TO MAKE

1 Fill the glass to the rim over the sink.

2 Place the piece of paper flat on the water.

3 Place your other hand flat on the paper then turn the glass over quickly.

4 Take your hand away: the paper suctions against the water and prevents it from spilling.

And you can
eat it!

MUSHROOMS
MADE OF MOZZARELLA AND TOMATOES

INGREDIENTS
MOZZARELLA BALLS
CHERRY TOMATOES
   (ELONGATED IN SHAPE, IF POSSIBLE)
COTTAGE CHEESE

HOW TO MAKE

1 Drain and wipe the mozzarella balls. Cut the base a bit so they will stand on their own.

2 Cut the cherry tomatoes in half. Empty out the pulp and position each tomato half on a mozzarella ball.

3 Place little dots of the cottage cheese on the tomatoes using a sharp knife.

SPAGHETTI NESTS
BAKED IN A MUFFIN PAN

INGREDIENTS
SPAGHETTI
GARNISHES (LIKE PEAS AND MINT LEAVES)
TOMATO MOZZARELLA SALAD
 SOFT CHEESE, PEARS & DRIED FRUIT

HOW TO MAKE
1 Cook the spaghetti in boiling water as instructed on the package. Drain well.

2 Arrange the noodles like nests in the muffin pan and bake them in a 350°F (180°C) oven for approximately 10 minutes.

3 Take them out of the pan once they have cooled: they will have hardened somewhat and taken on the shape of the pan. Garnish them with the ingredients that you've gathered and chopped up into small pieces. Serve cold.

ADORABLE RADISH MICE
WITH LONG TAILS

MATERIALS
RADISHES
POPPY OR MUSTARD SEEDS
A SHARP KNIFE

HOW TO MAKE

1 Choose radishes with the nicest roots.

2 Cut off the radish tops and cut the end of each radish into a point.

3 Cut out two small slits where the ears should be.

4 Cut out slim circles from another radish. Cut each circle in half to create two ears. Place them in the slits you created.

5 Press in the seeds to create the eyes.

MINIATURE GARDENS
MADE OF MUSHROOMS

HOW TO MAKE

1 Delicately peel the mushrooms with a paring knife. Cut off the stems.

2 Rub the half lemon onto the mushrooms to prevent them from browning.

3 Fill the cavities of the mushrooms with the cream cheese and smooth the surface.

4 Place one or more small herb sprigs into the cheese.

5 Break a few toothpicks in half and insert three halves into each mushroom to hold it up.

INGREDIENTS

WHITE MUSHROOMS
HALF A LEMON
CREAM CHEESE
AROMATIC HERBS

The palm tree is created by inserting a fennel sprig into a short piece of chive.

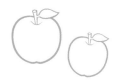

AN APPLE SPIRAL
DAZZLING IN MINUTES

MATERIALS

AN APPLE
A KNIFE
A TOOTHPICK

HOW TO MAKE

1 Cut the apple so you end up with a small half without any of the core. Cut off one-third of this piece.

2 Thinly slice the remaining piece.

3 Keep these slices in place with the help of the toothpick.

4 Separate the slices around the toothpick center to create a spiral.

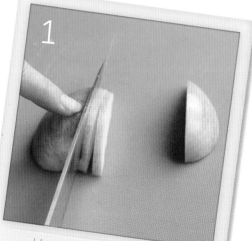

You can create two spirals out of one apple.

The toothpick center must be perfectly straight!

Let the dazzle begin!

113

My Neighbor Totoro
Made of Lychees

MATERIALS

A SHARP, FINE CUTTING TOOL
TWO LYCHEES
TWO CLOVES
SIX SPRIGS OF DRIED ROSEMARY
ONE TOOTHPICK
CORRECTION FLUID
A BLACK MARKER

HOW TO MAKE

1. With your cutting tool, cut out a circle in the bark of the first lychee to create the belly.

2. Push the two cloves into the lychee bark where the eyes should be. Draw a small white circle with the correction fluid on each clove, as well as a black dot with the marker in the center of each eye, and also for the nose.

3. Cut out two small spikes behind the eyes and straighten them to create the ears.

4. Create two small holes with the toothpick on either side of the nose. Insert a few sprigs of rosemary into each hole to create the whiskers.

5. Cut the other lychee in half, setting one-half of the shell aside. Turn it over delicately: it will become the umbrella, and it looks best on the pink, smooth side. Insert the toothpick into the shell and slide the handle of the umbrella into the hole of one of the ears.

となりのトトロ

A TEDDY BEAR PANCAKE
OR HOW TO DRAW IN A PAN

INGREDIENTS
3 EGGS
1⅞ CUPS (375 ML) WHEAT FLOUR
1 CUP (250 ML) MILK
2 TBSP (30 ML) POWDERED SUGAR
½ PACKAGE OF YEAST
POWDERED CHOCOLATE
HONEY OR MAPLE SYRUP

HOW TO MAKE

1 Separate the egg whites from the yolks and beat the whites until they're stiff and peaks form.

2 In a separate bowl, stir together the yolks, sugar, flour and yeast. Add in the milk a little at a time, and then fold in the egg whites.

3 Place a little of the batter into another bowl and mix in some powdered chocolate.

4 Heat a medium-sized pan over medium heat. Using an eyedropper (like the type provided with children's medication), draw the bear's nose in the pan.

5 Cover the nose with the chocolate batter by forming a small oval then draw the contour of the head, ears, eyes and eyebrows, all with the eyedropper.

6 Using a small spoon, cover these drawings with the white batter.

7 Flip over the pancake as soon as bubbles start forming in the batter and cook for a few more moments on the other side. Serve with butter and honey or maple syrup.

The trick is to use an eyedropper to create the detailed drawings.

Cover everything with the white batter, and when you flip it over, it's magnificent!

A MELON CAGE
WITH A PEAR-FENNEL BIRD

HOW TO MAKE

1 Insert two cloves into the pear to create the eyes.

2 Carefully remove layers from the fennel. They will become smaller and smaller. Stop once you have one that is the same size as the pear. Cut off the stems as needed. Adjust it to fit the pear.

3 Cut off a bit of the base of the melon so that it can stand up on its own, then cut it in half to create a base and a roof. Empty out the seeds and the pulp from the roof (to make it lighter), leaving a rim around the edge that will be used to hold the bars of the cage.

4 Push the wooden skewers into the base. Cover the hole that was holding the seeds with a saucer. Place the bird on it. Adjust the roof by pushing it into the wooden picks.

5 Hollow out the fennel heart to create a small, deep bowl. Put seeds in it and place it in the cage.

MATERIALS

CLOVES
A SMALL PEAR
A FENNEL BULB
A MELON
WOODEN SKEWERS
A KNIFE
A SPOON
A SMALL SAUCER
BIRD SEED

The hardest part is convincing yourself that it's OK to eat the bird and cage.

118

AN ORIGAMI CAKE
BAKED IN FOLDED PARCHMENT PAPER

❖

MATERIALS
CAKE BATTER (OF YOUR CHOICE)
A SQUARE PIECE OF PARCHMENT PAPER

HOW TO MAKE

1 Mark the folds of the diagonals on one side, and of the midpoints on the other, to enable you to fold the piece of parchment and end up with a square like the one shown in diagram 1.

2 Fold down two triangles towards the center, as shown in diagram 2.

3 Open and flatten these triangles (diagram 3), then turn over and do the same on the other side.

4 Fold the four diamonds toward the outside following the vertical axis (diagram 4).

5 Mark the fold indicated in diagram 5: this will be the base of the mold.

6 Fold the bottom point toward the top by following the line of diagram 6.

7 Fold the top layer of the shape like you would the page of a book: you'll end up with a shape like the one in diagram 6.

8 Push on the base to open the folds: you now have a box. Next, pour the batter into the box and bake the cake in the oven. To unmold, simply pull on the four points.

1   2   3

4   5   6   7

AN ALPHABET NOODLE STAMP
AND A HEART-SHAPED COOKIE CUTTER

MATERIALS

ALPHABET PASTA
A LARGE CORK
GLUE
A PIECE OF TRANSPARENT THIN PLASTIC
SCISSORS
A STAPLER (OR ADHESIVE TAPE)
SHORTBREAD DOUGH

HOW TO MAKE

1 To make the stamp, choose the letters in the bag of pasta to create the word that you want. Glue the letters upside down on the cork, as if you were reading in a mirror. Allow the glue to completely dry.

2 To make the heart-shaped cookie cutter, cut out a band of plastic, fold it in half and join the ends to form a heart. Hold it closed with a stapler (or tape).

3 Unroll and spread the dough. Create hearts with the cookie cutter then mark the dough hearts with the stamp.

4 Bake the cookies in the oven at 350°F (180°C) for approximately 10 minutes.

It's very easy to salvage a piece of plastic to create the heart shape.

The stamp can be used on dough or play dough.

A PIÑATA CAKE
WITH CANDY HIDDEN INSIDE

MATERIALS

A METAL SALAD BOWL OR CAKE MOLD
ALUMINUM FOIL
A GRAPEFRUIT
THREE TOOTHPICKS
PREPARED CAKE BATTER
   (FROM A MIX OR YOGURT CAKE RECIPE)
FROSTING
CANDY
DECORATIONS

The piñata before it's been cut into. Surprise!

HOW TO MAKE

1 Wrap the bowl or cake mold with aluminum foil to make unmolding the cake as easy as possible. Wrap the grapefruit in aluminum foil as well. Insert three toothpicks into the grapefruit to create a tripod that will hold the grapefruit in the cake mold.

2 Pour the cake batter into the mold and bake the cake.

3 When the cake is baked and has cooled off, unmold it and take out the grapefruit. Fill the cavity with candy and turn the cake upside down.

4 Cover the cake with frosting and decorations, such as candy cut into slices

The "Sputnik" grapefruit..

The cake will rise
around the grapefruit.

Voila! All that's left to do is take out
the grapefruit to create a hole.

The unmolded cake with candy hidden
inside. All that's missing is the frosting!

SMALL REMINDERS

YOGURT CAKE

INGREDIENTS

A 140G (5 OZ) POT OF YOGURT
A HALF POT OF OIL
TWO POTS OF SUGAR
THREE POTS OF FLOUR
TWO EGGS
HALF A PACKAGE OF YEAST
SOMETHING TO FLAVOR THE CAKE
    TO YOUR LIKING, SUCH AS LEMON ZEST
    OR CHOCOLATE CHIPS

*Tip: Use the yogurt pot to measure
        out the flour, sugar and oil*

WHITE FROSTING

INGREDIENTS

½ CUP (125 ML) PLAIN CREAM CHEESE
THE JUICE OF HALF A LEMON
½ CUP (125 ML) ICING SUGAR

A PIÑATA, WHAT'S THAT?

It's a Mexican tradition: a piñata is a large empty object made out of a breakable material (typically papier-mâché) that blindfolded children try to break open at a party to release the hidden treasures inside.

AN ANGEL HAIR NEST
TO TOP A CAKE

When the professionals make spun sugar, they let the temperature rise to 330°F (165°C).

The setup to create angel hair — a somewhat difficult operation!

MATERIALS

POWDERED OR CASTER SUGAR
A FRYING PAN
A FORK
PARCHMENT PAPER
TWO LONG HANDLES
    (FOR EXAMPLE, WOODEN SPOON HANDLES)

HOW TO MAKE

1 Prepare your workspace so that the two wooden spoon handles are horizontal, pointing toward you, approximately 12 inches (30 cm) above a workspace that's been covered with parchment paper.

2 Cover the bottom of the frying pan with powdered or caster sugar. Let it melt at medium heat without stirring until it resembles caramel. It must be liquid, but not too runny. You will need to reheat the melted sugar throughout the process to obtain the ideal consistency.

3 Pour the caramel onto the two suspended handles with the help of a fork, going from one handle to the other. Fine "threads" will form from the cooling caramel.

4 Take these threads in your hand and form a nest before they become too dry and breakable.

129

A SWARM OF EDIBLE BUTTERFLIES
TO DECORATE A CAKE

MATERIALS
A BUTTERFLY SHAPED HOLE PUNCH
A FILO PASTRY SHEET
ICING SUGAR
TOOTHPICKS

HOW TO MAKE

1 Using the hole punch, cut out the butterflies from the filo pastry sheet.

2 Place the butterflies on a sheet of silicone or a piece of parchment paper. Dust with icing sugar. Bake for 5 minutes in a 350°F (180°C) oven.

3 Decorate the cake: create small slits with a knife and slide the butterflies into them. Hang others on toothpicks. Balance the last butterflies off the first ones you placed. (Be careful, they are very fragile!)

You can find patterned hole punches in craft supply stores.

A CAROUSEL CAKE
WITH HAZELNUTS AND LOLLIPOPS

INGREDIENTS & MATERIALS

AN EMPTY PLASTIC BOTTLE
TWO STOREBOUGHT HAZELNUT
  CAKES (IN THEIR PACKAGING)
CANDY
PLASTIC WRAP
8 SMALL LOLLIPOPS
SMALL TOY ANIMALS

HOW TO MAKE

1 Cut the plastic bottle, keeping only the top section, which will serve as the central axis for the carousel.

2 Take the cakes out of their packaging. Pierce one cake with the cut bottle and put aside the small cylinder of cake.

3 Fill the bottle with candy and seal it with plastic wrap. Wedge it, standing up, into the hole of the bottom cake.

4 Turn over one of the cardboard cake trays and make eight small holes around the perimeter to slide the lollipops into. Pierce the center of the cake tray with a knife, creating two slits that will form an X the size of the bottle cap.

5 Put the turned-over cake tray on the bottle and place the second cake on top of it. Insert the lollipops upside down into the holes of the cardboard tray.

6 Decorate the roof with the small cylinder of cake you saved from earlier, and some candy. Insert small animals into the cake at the base of the carousel.

The half-bottle filled with candy serves as the support for the second story.

Happy Birthday!

PINECONE SYRUP
THAT TASTES LIKE MAPLE SYRUP

MATERIALS
SOME GREEN PINECONES
POWDERED OR CASTER SUGAR
SEVERAL JARS

HOW TO MAKE

1 Pick some pinecones while they are still green. Carefully check that there aren't any creatures living inside!

2 Fill each jar with alternating layers of powdered or caster sugar and pinecones. Place in the refrigerator to prevent them from becoming moldy.

3 Wait patiently for about one month: the cones will release a resin that will dissolve the sugar. The syrup will be ready to eat when it is completely liquefied.

The sight of the sugar melting around the cones is an exercise in patience.

Delicious on pancakes or
with cottage cheese.

THE PHASES OF THE MOON
MADE FROM SANDWICH COOKIES

MATERIALS
SEVEN SANDWICH COOKIES
A SHARP KNIFE

HOW TO MAKE

1 Open up the cookies without damaging the cream filling.

2 Put aside the half of the cookie without filling on it to create the nights without a moon, and the half with the filling untouched to create the full moon.

3 Using the knife, scrape the filling from the other cookies to represent the different phases of the moon.

new moon

waxing crescent

waning crescent

first quarter

t quarter

waning gibbous

waxing gibbous

full moon

HOW TO AMAZE YOUR SON

How to make fake snow

A ghost

A house in a cardboard tree

Playmobil® ice pops

A gummy bear catapult

140

A tree house built
in broccoli

A small door that
hides an
electrical outlet

Balls of ice with
lights inside

A shark
pencil case

A drum kit made of tin cans

A campfire cake

141

THEMATIC INDEX
SELECTED

ALPHABETICAL INDEX

THANK YOUS

Thank you to my daughter **Avril** for her help on numerous pages, for making figures and especially for her perpetual enthusiasm. Thank you to the other children who posed or helped: **Rose, Ida, Maïa, Philomene** and **Félix.**
Thank you to my mother **Bernadette**, who still amazes me at my age: she made the beach chairs for the dolls, the mermaid costume, the matchbox huts, the teepees and the table tent.
Thank you to **Corine**, who drew the characters on the pebbles and the decorations for the laundry jug house, and who made, with **Francis**, the foldable cardboard house.
Thank you to **Loran, Yves, Léa** and **Rémi**, who helped with the photographs.

Text, photos and layout: Raphaële Vidaling
Cover creation: Marina Delranc
Photo engraving: Peggy Huynh-Quan-Suu
Book produced by Copyright

144